Original title:
Island Echoes

Copyright © 2025 Creative Arts Management OÜ
All rights reserved.

Author: Rory Fitzgerald
ISBN HARDBACK: 978-1-80581-671-3
ISBN PAPERBACK: 978-1-80581-198-5
ISBN EBOOK: 978-1-80581-671-3

Whispers of the Forgotten Shore

Seagulls gossip about the beach,
They squawk about a sandy peach.
The crabs dance like they own the scene,
While sunburnt tourists cling to sunscreen.

A coconut fell on a silly man's hat,
He swore it was a surprise from a cat.
The waves chuckled as they came to play,
While beach towels turned to sail away.

Tides of Silent Reminiscence

A flip-flop flop rings out like a bell,
The waves giggle, 'What stories to tell?'
Old shells whisper how they once knew,
A starfish that thought it could surf too.

Sunbathers compete in the sandball game,
While sunscreen wars erupt, who's to blame?
Under umbrellas, laughter flies high,
As a seagull steals a hot dog nearby.

The Call of Distant Horizons

A fisherman dreams of a catch so grand,
But his line is tangled in a child's hand.
The boat's a ship of ridiculous dreams,
Sailing off with sunlight in its beams.

Mermaids giggle at the sight below,
Swapping tales with the waves in a flow.
"Is it lunchtime?" an old sailor creaks,
While dolphins laugh, and everyone sneaks.

Reverberations Beneath the Coconut Trees

Under coconuts, the crickets sing,
While a dog tries to fetch a coconut ring.
The palm trees sway, holding secrets old,
Of the goofy tourists and tales they told.

A lizard struts like he owns the place,
With sunglasses perched on his tiny face.
As the sun sets to a calypso beat,
The night brings out tales of friends to meet.

Whispers in the Coral Maze

In the maze where fish go sing,
A crab wears bling, it's quite the thing.
Turtles giggle at a seaweed prank,
Meanwhile, the octopus is drawing blank.

The seahorses dance on ocean's floor,
While clams are snoozing, craving more.
A starfish stumbles, lost in the show,
As bubbles rise where the currents flow.

The Quietude Between Waves

Between the rolls, a dolphin snorts,
With a splash, he starts funny sports.
Seagulls squawking in silly debates,
While starfish toast with champagne plates.

A pelican's dive is always a mess,
He lands on a boat, much to their stress.
Fish are chuckling, caught in the game,
In the lull, it's never the same.

Luminescence in the Twilight Surf

In twilight's glow, the jellyfish beam,
They light up the night like a crazy dream.
Crabs on the shore have a limbo race,
While shells roll around, keeping pace.

The moon cackles on the silver sea,
As seaweed wiggles with glee, whee!
Waves whisper secrets, tickling the night,
Under the stars, everything feels right.

Dreams Cast Adrift in the Currents

Drifting dreams through salty air,
A fish holds court, all is fair.
Anemones giggle, swaying to the beat,
While snails parade, it's quite the feat.

The sea laughs softly at the clownfish's show,
As they tell tales of the waters below.
A sand dollar jokes, 'I'm quite the star,'
In currents they dream, oh, how bizarre.

Secrets Carried by the Breeze

A whisper rides upon the wind,
The crabs recount their tales of sin.
Seagulls squawk in surgeon's glee,
As waves play tricks upon the spree.

The coconut laughs in the sun's embrace,
While a tiny fish dances in a silly race.
The breeze tells jokes that make us grin,
As the old boat creaks, let the fun begin!

A parrot mimics a toddler's cry,
While a lazy dog lets out a sigh.
Ears perked up from the breeze's flow,
It's comedy hour, front-row show!

As bananas slip and monkeys swing,
On sandcastles, laughter does ring.
What secrets does the wind conspire?
Finding treasures in laughter's fire.

Murmurs Beneath the Palm Canopy

Under palm leaves, the shadows play,
A lizard prances in a charming way.
The breeze brings jokes from far-off lands,
And tickles the toes of shed-sand hands.

Squirrels gossip about nuts gone missing,
While old sea turtles just sit, reminiscing.
The sun has jokes, though it's a bit bright,
Dancing shadows leap in sheer delight!

A crab in a hat struts with flair,
While nearby a dolphin waves from the air.
Whispers of waves blend laughter and grace,
Every murmured secret finds its place.

As children build castles with care,
They find that fun is everywhere.
With smiles shared and silly plays,
Beneath palm leaves, joy sways.

Songs of Solitude in the Sea

A lonely shell sings a tune so sweet,
To fish who gather for a lunch-time treat.
Crabby comedians practice their lines,
While dolphins giggle at dripping designs.

A lone seaweed begins to dance,
Its moves are bold, as if by chance.
The waves join in on this silly spree,
As pearls chuckle, wishing to be free!

A fish in a bowtie takes center stage,
With soft seafoam laughing like a page.
The tide brings chuckles, and laughter flows,
As songs of solitude cut through the prose.

A driftwood orchestra plays so grand,
To the rhythm of waves on the sand.
Even the ocean can crack a smile,
As silliness stretches for quite a while.

Echoes of Distant Horizons

In the sunset glow, echoes arise,
A crab sings ballads, oh, what a surprise!
The horizon stretches, giggling afar,
As sea monsters blush beneath a star.

Laughter spills over the waves like foam,
While distant shores call the boats back home.
Sardines in a choir harmonize the breeze,
Filling the night with songs that appease.

The horizon teases with tickling mist,
As the playful tides form a light-hearted twist.
Every echo a secret, a joke wrapped tight,
Filling our souls with glee every night.

What fun awaits in the twilight glow,
As whispers and giggles start to flow.
The world spins on with a chuckling call,
In the echoes of humor, we find our all.

The Calm Before the Storm

The sun shines bright, a playful tease,
While waves prepare their big caprice,
  Seagulls squawk with comic flair,
    As I lose my hat in salty air.

Bikini tops fly like flags of war,
Kids run fast to touch the shore,
A splash like laughter fills the air,
And out comes the brave dog, unaware.

Nature's Silent Rhapsody

Fluffy clouds of cotton candy,
Whispers soft, yet oh so dandy,
Turtles race, but who will win?
A crab just winked, a gentle grin.

I measure banter by the tide,
Fish wiggling, giving me a ride,
Algae dances, frothy jokes,
Nature's laughter somehow evokes.

Trails of the Wandering Gulls

Gulls swoop low, in search of fries,
Dodging old men and crying cries,
They squawk and squabble, quite the scene,
Like acrobats, they strut and preen.

A seagull drops a sandwich far,
While tourists giggle, shout, and spar,
Their impromptu show makes me grin,
I might just join, let chaos begin!

Tides of Memory

Footprints washed away like dreams,
As I recall old ice cream screams,
Sandcastles tumble, giggles loud,
We danced around, a silly crowd.

Much time has passed since those wild days,
But antics linger in sunny rays,
A crab now waves, what a rogue,
It shimmies like it's part of the vogue!

Shifts of Time

Time shifts like the sand beneath,
From childish games to surfer's wreath,
We leap and spin like stones on water,
With every laugh, life's sweetly hotter.

The sun sets low, the day retreats,
Tickling waves in friendly beats,
A night of tales like stars unfold,
As we roast marshmallows, brave and bold!

Reflections of a Solitary Dream

A coconut fell with a loud thud,
"I'm fine!" I yelled, like a real stud.
The crabs all giggled, oh what a show,
As I danced like a fish, trying not to glow.

The sun wore sunglasses, cool and bright,
While seagulls squawked, "You're not quite right!"
I posed like a star in a comedy skit,
The palm trees swayed, laughing at my wit.

A wave rolled in, whispered, "Hey you!"
I splashed back, saying, "That tickles too!"
The tide joined in with a bubbly cheer,
We made a splash, laughter in the clear.

As the day ended with a wink and a spin,
I tipped my hat, said, "Let the fun begin!"
The night sky giggled with stars in a row,
My dream floated on, casting jokes down below.

The Language of Distant Shores

On shores afar, where the sand meets the tide,
I spoke to a clam, with nowhere to hide.
"What's the gossip?" I asked with a grin,
It winked back softly, "You wouldn't fit in!"

The waves whispered secrets, some funny, some true,
A starfish chimed in, "We all thought of you!"
With laughter like bubbles, I danced on the sand,
While seashells chuckled, caught in my hand.

The gulls held a meeting, in circles they flew,
"Forget about fish, what's next on the menu?"
I joined in the fun, a conch as my microphone,
Turns out my jokes were better alone!

As sunset painted pink, I waved to the sea,
The tide rolled back, laughing at me.
In this world of whimsy, I found my place,
Among creatures who giggle, and love to embrace.

Songs of the Wanderlust Waves

The ocean's a stage, where waves come to play,
They flip and they flop, in a watery ballet.
With every big splash, they send out a call,
"Come join us, dear friend, for a dance and a brawl!"

The surfboards are laughing, as they ride the crest,
"Who can stay upright? Come put us to the test!"
I tried and I wobbled, oh what a sight,
The sea whispered softly, "You're doing it right!"

A dolphin swam by, with a wink and a spin,
"Join us for fun, let the games begin!"
With flips and with flops, we made quite the scene,
Sailing through giggles, bright and serene.

As the moon shone down, a silver delight,
We danced 'neath the stars, through the warm summer night.
The waves sang their songs, so silly and sweet,
The wanderlust waves, a silly heartbeat.

Tales of the Celestial Drift

The stars above twinkled, wearing mischief's grin,
They whispered to me, "Let the stories begin!"
I sat on my floatie, sipping some air,
While the sunbeams chuckled, it was quite a pair.

The moon was a joker, with a cheeky wink,
"Tell me your dreams, what do you think?"
I shared my wild tales, of cats sailing boats,
And fish wearing hats, in glittery coats.

Each wave brought a giggle, a nudge from behind,
"Hey, don't be shy, let the fun unwind!"
Together we laughed, with the stars as our crowd,
In this celestial drift, joy felt so loud.

As the night drifted by, wrapped in twinkling light,
I knew these tall tales would last through the night.
With every soft ripple, more laughter would swell,
On this floating stage, we had tales to tell.

Echos of the Ancient Mariner

A seagull cackles, quite in jest,
As sailors ponder, where's the rest?
With fish as friends and rum as cheer,
They swear a whale just swam near here!

Old tales spun, with laughter loud,
About the shark that scared the crowd.
They sip their grog, while tales unfold,
Of treasures sought, or so we're told!

A pirate's grin, a parrot's shout,
Mix up the maps, and then we're out!
To find the trove of silly dreams,
And laugh at how the ocean gleams!

With every wave, a goofy dance,
The crew's antics lead to a chance.
To jest and jibe beneath the sun,
The sailor's life is all in fun!

Reflections of a Forgotten Voyage

Upon the waves, a mirror cracked,
Reminds of snacks we surely lacked.
The captain sneezes, sails go boom,
A fish jumps high into the gloom!

We once forgot the maps we drew,
Instead, we sailed where mermaids blew.
With laughter loud and chips to munch,
A seaweed salad for our lunch!

The stars above make dolphins laugh,
While humor leads the silly craft.
We dance and sing in salty air,
Our voyage's worth the goofy flair!

And in the night, the laughter thrived,
As all those fish tales came alive.
We share a toast with every wave,
To this lost trip we all can save!

The Softness of the Sea's Caress

The ocean hugs with gentle waves,
Tickles toes, and how it braves!
With jellyfish that float and glide,
We giggle as they swim beside!

A crab in shorts, so very rare,
Dances 'round without a care.
While clams compose a silly tune,
Swaying softly beneath the moon!

The sea breeze whispers cheeky jokes,
While seagulls chat like merry folks.
And sunscreen's smarts bring lots of grins,
As we avoid the burning sins!

With every splash and giggle shared,
The waves remind us we all dared.
So here's to fun where laughter flows,
In the embrace where sea grass grows!

Stories Drifted on the Wind

A breeze brings tales from far away,
Of pirates lost who went astray.
With every gust, the tales unwind,
Of treasure chests that love to hide!

The gales will tease, with puns so sly,
As gulls above just dance and fly.
Their antics make the sailors chuckle,
While dodging splashes, what a struggle!

Old sails creak, as stories share,
Of fish that wear a comical flair.
And every wave that crashes loud,
Brings out the joyful, raucous crowd!

So let the winds inspire our laughs,
As we recount our silly paths.
With every breeze, new tales we weave,
In the laughter that we believe!

Tales from Beneath the Sea Foam

A crab wore a hat, quite snug and neat,
He danced on the sand, with two left feet.
The fish laughed aloud, in bubbles of mirth,
As seaweed did sway, a wobbly birth.

A clam told a joke, with a shellfish grin,
But the octopus just couldn't join in.
He had too many arms, a ticklish source,
And wound up in knots, like a wild horse.

A turtle with shades, claimed he was fast,
But slowly crept by, and the day slipped past.
The seagulls all squawked, "You're pulling our fins!"
As he caught up to fish, with jellybean skins.

In the depths, tales swirl, a giggle afloat,
With sea critters laughing, on each little note.

Reverberations among the Cliffs

The gulls made a racket, all shrieks and caws,
They plotted to steal a crab's just-cooked claws.
But the crab, wise as ever, played a sly trick,
He served up a feast, a buffet so thick.

A dolphin once laughed, as waves threw her high,
But landed near barnacles, oh my, oh my!
Stuck tight in a tussle, she'd wiggle and twist,
"Next time I'll jump, with a much smaller list!"

The seal, clad in shades, sunbathed with such flair,
Claiming sea breeze was best done without care.
But a wave came to splash, sending him in flight,
He yelped as he flipped, a comical sight!

Chasing echoes so loud, as friendships would bloom,
Among cliffs that jump, laughter filled every room.

Harmonies of the Sheltered Cove

A sea turtle crooned, 'bout the tides and the stars,
While starfish joined in, playing old guitars.
They jammed on the rocks, with shells as their stage,
Creating a tune that danced off the page.

The minnows did wiggle, in synchronized steps,
They twirled through the bubbles, avoiding missteps.
But one little fish, with a big dreamy sigh,
Got dizzy from spinning, and straight up flew by!

A wise old whale hummed, with depth and delight,
As the sun painted hues, igniting the night.
Yet a barnacle snored, in a deep, gentle way,
Soft serenades echoing, ending the day.

In this cove of tales, where laughter plays loud,
The sea creatures frolic, forever unbowed.

Whirlpools of Time and Memory

A whirlpool once whispered, 'Take a dip, have fun!'
But the fish shook their heads, 'We'd prefer the sun.'
Yet a brave little shrimp, full of sprightly flair,
Dove in with a splash, flinging water everywhere.

The eels had a party, all slick and amazed,
With electric dance moves, they dazzled the bays.
But a grouchy old rockfish, grumbled in haste,
"I prefer my stillness; this whirlpool's a waste!"

Time does indeed whirl, with laughter and cheer,
As memories spin, and the past feels quite near.
The sea's a great jester, with splashes and glee,
Where every wave whispers, "Just float, you'll be free!"

Through ups and downs, oh, the stories we share,
In whirlpools of joy, let your worries all spare.

Hymns to the Boundless Sky

Oh look at the birds, how they dance and spin,
With feathers that shimmer, they make me grin.
They dive for a fish, but catch just a shoe,
A lesson in fishing, they clearly outgrew.

The clouds are large pillows, they float and they play,
While the sun wears a hat, it brightens the day.
A rainbow's a slide for the colors to ride,
And the rain, well, that's just a wet water slide.

Driftwood and the Sound of Silence

There's driftwood that whispers, or so it is said,
It tells tales of dolphins and a crab who fled.
A hermit crab scolds with quite a loud snap,
While a seagull laughs loudly, 'You're stuck in that gap!'

The sand giggles softly, tickling toes,
While seashells gossip about where the tide goes.
A clam dreams of swimming, it's quite a surprise,
But it's content just sitting, hiding away in disguise.

The Forgotten Pulse of the Deep

Beneath the warm waves, an octopus plays,
With eight silly limbs, it dances in bays.
It wiggles and jigs with a toothy old grin,
As starfish do cartwheels, and fish join in like kin.

The seaweed is swaying, performing its show,
While crabs hold a meeting, 'What do we know?'
With bubbles as tunes, and the current as beat,
They tap-dance together, all wiggly and sweet.

Cacophony of the Wind-swept Dunes

The wind loves to yell, it's a boisterous thing,
It tugs at my hat with a mischievous fling.
A tumbleweed rolls by with a laugh and a cheer,
While I dodge sandstorms like a cowboy, oh dear!

The dunes start to giggle with every light breeze,
As lizards parade, wearing jackets of cheese.
The sun sets in colors that splash and collide,
As shadows do dance in a joyride slide.

Sighs of the Serene Lagoon

A parrot sings with sassy flair,
While fish play tag without a care.
The crabs dance sideways on the sand,
A conch shell giggles, he's the band.

A turtle yawns, then takes a dive,
While jellyfish do a wobbly jive.
The seaweed sways in rhythm sweet,
As dolphins practice their funny feet.

Reflections on the Tranquil Waters

A frog in shades just croaks a tune,
The sun begins to peek by noon.
A duck quacks jokes about the breeze,
While algae floats, oh what a tease!

The heron sways and tries to dance,
While fish giggle, given the chance.
The ripples laugh at all the fuss,
As bubbles pop with playful thrust.

The Heartbeat of the Distant Reef

A clownfish bursts with polka dots,
It cracks a smile, and laughs a lot.
The sea cucumbers talk so slow,
While an octopus puts on a show.

Corals blush in vibrant light,
While urchins share their quips all night.
The starfish giggles, five limbs splayed,
As they whisper jokes in watery shade.

Chants of the Wandering Waves

The waves roll in with a silly grin,
They tickle the shore, inviting kin.
A seagull glides on an airborne joke,
While sandcastles moan, 'We're going to choke!'

The tide swirls back to tickle toes,
As crabs tell tales of forgotten woes.
Salty breezes join in the fun,
For laughter reigns when day is done.

Glistening Castaways of Time

We found a bottle, it had a stout,
Inside a note, asking for a spout.
A map to treasure, or so we thought,
Just led to seashells, which we then fought.

Sunburnt dreams mixed with sandy laughter,
A crab stole our snacks, running faster.
We chased it down, what a wild race,
For crumbs of bread, we'd lost our grace.

In the distance, a parrot gave cheer,
Gossiping tales we barely could hear.
It squawked about mates lost at sea,
Turns out it was just a plea for tea.

So here we are, with our kitschy finds,
Wandering waves, with goofy minds.
A treasure chest filled with giggles vast,
In this swirling whirlpool, we had a blast.

An Overture of Water and Silence

The tides applauded in a soft hush,
While we set up camp, amidst the rush.
A fish flicked its tail, causing a splash,
And soaked our picnic—oh what a clash!

We tried to grill, but the flames had died,
Instead we roasted marshmallows fried.
The smoke danced up, tickling our noses,
Leaving behind a scent like old roses.

A seal popped up, wagging its chin,
Caught us chuckling, as it dove in.
We serenaded it, but it just yawned,
And with that grin, our song betrayed and dawned.

So we sang to the waves, trying to reign,
While they responded with a melodic refrain.
Laughter echoed through the salty mist,
In this whirl of joy, we couldn't resist.

Shadows at Dusk on the Cove

When shadows grew long, we felt quite bold,
We danced with the crabs, quite a sight to behold.
Their sideways shuffle was a real delight,
We laughed and jigged until the night.

A sunset surprise, glowing shades of red,
Our dance floor lit, we spun 'til we fled.
The gulls joined in, trying to steal the show,
But we were the stars, as we put on a glow.

The tide rolled in, with whispers and sways,
We tripped on the waves, in comical displays.
Fell in the sand, our giggles took flight,
Two sunburnt comedians, under the moonlight.

And as night draped, in dark blues and blacks,
We swore to return, back on our tracks.
For tales of the cove carried on quite grand,
With shadows still dancing, hand in hand.

Spheric Amulets of Forgotten Tales

Round and round, the ball did bounce,
From kid to kid, with a friendly pounce.
We thought it was magic, or maybe a curse,
As it rolled away, our luck got worse.

A seagull swooped down, or maybe three,
Took our lunch, oh what calamity!
They chattered and squawked, a feathery theft,
Stealing our sandwiches, that was quite deft.

Shells became hats, and driftwoods swords,
Pirate games played with fervent chords.
We raided the beach, with giggles and screams,
Lost in a world of imaginative dreams.

So here's to the joys of sun and sand,
Of treasures imagined, oh so grand.
Laughter forged nets, to catch every breeze,
In this realm of mirth, we found our peace.

Captured Moments Beneath the Stars

Under the sky, a stray sock flies,
Caught in the breeze, oh how it tries.
Dancing like jelly, not a care in sight,
Laughter erupts, oh what a night!

Crabs in the sand, hosting a ball,
Pinching toes, they're having a ball!
Stars are giggling, casting their light,
We toast with coconuts, cheers to the night!

Bicycles rusted, forgotten and bent,
Reckless joy on journeys, laughter unspent.
Chasing the sun, we run and we race,
Punching gulls playfully, giving them chase!

In the distance, the moon starts to sway,
Singing a tune, "Come join the play!"
With each echoing chuckle, our antics take flight,
Captured moments beneath the stars, what a sight!

The Cerulean Echo of Yesterdays

A flip-flop flies, what a daring feat,
Chasing a breeze, taking to the street.
Maracas rattle on a sunlit shore,
Dance, dance, dance! Who could want more?

Seagulls conspire, with mischievous croaks,
Plotting and planning, oh, what a hoax!
Tales of old splashes from years gone by,
Fish that leapt high, just to wave goodbye!

A parrot named Lou, with jokes up his sleeve,
Tells of a time when I dared to weave.
Knots in my hair from a sunset ride,
Rolling in laughter, with naught left to hide!

Waves echo whispers of days we once knew,
Full of mischief and pineapple stew.
Under the sun, we jest and we play,
With cerulean dreams drifting far away!

Whispers of the Forgotten Shore

Shells sing secrets of long-lost tales,
Echoing laughter like ships with sails.
Forgotten treasures buried in sand,
We dig and we laugh, life feels so grand.

A crab wearing shades, oh what a sight!
Dancing in rhythm, oh what a night!
Tangled in seaweed, we trip and we fall,
In the end, it's a wild, wacky ball!

Jellyfish float like balloons in the air,
Wiggling and jiggling, without a care.
The sun sneezes bright; we run for the shade,
Trading our secrets, oh, what a brigade!

The waves reminisce songs of our youth,
Each splash a reminder, have fun in truth.
Whispers of joys from the depths of the shore,
Promising laughter, and so much more!

Lullabies of the Tides

Tides hum a tune on a lazy day,
While crabs on the rocks start to sway.
Beach towels flying, oh what a dance,
With sand in our hair, we take a chance!

A dolphin leaps, just to show off,
Splashes of water, a playful scoff.
Mermaids giggle, with jokes to unfold,
Sharing their laughter, as stories are told.

Seashells now whisper, each one a gem,
Secrets of tides wrapped up in a hem.
The sun starts to set, curtains drawn tight,
But joy doesn't fade, it returns every night!

With lullabies sung of waves' soft embrace,
We find all our worries have vanished without trace.
Moments of fun, as the tides pull away,
We promise to come back, to play another day!

The Call of Distant Shores

On a boat made of dreams, I drift,
Chasing crabs, they give me the lift.
Seagulls squawking with much delight,
Stealing my fries in broad daylight.

Palm trees waving, they seem to dance,
Each wave whispers, here's your chance.
I've lost my hat to the gusty breeze,
It sails away like it's off to tease.

Shells scream secrets, oh what a treat,
I trip on the sand and lose my feet.
The sun's too bright for a sly sunburn,
But it's all laughs, beyond concern.

In the distance, a distant cheer,
A beach ball flies, and I duck in fear.
With laughter rippling like the tide,
Fun awaits, here's where we hide!

Ethereal Songs of Combing Waves

Waves hum tunes, as I comb the shore,
Laughter bubbles like a fizzy pour.
With each swoosh, I find a lost flip-flop,
Are they my size? This saga won't stop!

Crabs in tuxedos, they waddle right,
Offering jokes, they're quite the sight.
Seashells gossip under the sun's glare,
Come join the fun—if you dare!

A sunhat flutters away on a dare,
Chasing it down, I tumble with flair.
Mermaids chuckle just out of reach,
Do they know I'm the star of this beach?

The tide sings songs of a twisty tune,
Under a sky of a bright cartoon.
So here's my heart laid bare on the sand,
With giggles and fun, oh isn't it grand?

Memories Grained in the Sand

Footprints tell tales, as we trip and fall,
I'm the king of the beach, or so I call.
With buckets of laughter, we dig down deep,
Finding treasures in waves that never sleep.

Seashells rolling, they play hard to get,
Every scooped one is a tiny bet.
The surf splashes back, a playful tease,
While I bend down, just to seize those keys!

With friends by my side, we build our dreams,
While seagulls plot in their crafty schemes.
A jellyfish dances, oh what a show,
But I'd rather dance, not lose my toe!

We share our stories, dripping with sand,
Every tale's funnier, growing up grand.
As the sun sets low and laughs start to fade,
Memories linger, never to trade!

Reflections at the Edge of the Deep

Peeking in waters, my face appears,
But it looks like a squid, oh dear, my peers!
With goggles strapped tight, I take a dive,
What a sight, this fishy jive!

Waves slap my cheeks with playful glee,
As dolphins laugh at the sight of me.
Turtles roll by with a lazy grin,
What's your secret, how do you win?

Flippers flapping, my dance is a whirl,
A crab waltzes by in a spunky twirl.
The ocean's a stage, and we play our part,
Each splash a curtain call to the heart.

As the night falls, stars wink and blink,
I sit with a smile, perched on the brink.
The fun lingers on, like a warm summer breeze,
With the ocean's soft whispers, we're always at ease!

Secrets of the Sunlit Cove

In a cove where sunbeams play,
The crabs hold dance-offs every day.
A parrot laughs with a cheeky grin,
While starfish sing, "Let the fun begin!"

Sea turtles race, oh what a sight,
With snorkelers cheering all through the night.
Seashells giggle, tucked in their beds,
Waves rolling in, tickling our heads.

But watch out for the jellyfish crew,
They throw a party—just for a few.
They bounce like rubber, with no care at all,
While dolphins dive, painting each call.

Here we toast with coconut drink,
And wonder if the octopus can think.
"Did you hear the one about the sea hare?"
"His punchline was, nobody was there!"

Memories Carried by the Sea Breeze

Fluffy clouds like cotton candy fly,
While seagulls squawk and swoop on by.
A crab wearing shades struts with flair,
While starfish giggle, "Oh, can you bear?"

The fish throw a party in water so blue,
Dancing around like they just grew.
An octopus dons a vibrant bow tie,
While mermaids sing and ninjas fly by.

Flip-flops flop as we race down the shore,
Hopping like frogs, who needs to explore?
The breeze whispers tales of giggles and dreams,
While waves shared secrets, or so it seems.

We reminisce about the jellyfish flare,
With tales that make us gasp and stare.
"Is it true they glow?" one friend inquired,
"Only when tickled—then they're wired!"

Shadows on the Coral Sand

A crab in a hat, what a sight for me,
Telling stories of captain and sea.
The shadows dance, twist left and right,
As fish do yoga, "It feels just right!"

The sands are warm like a big soft hug,
While a clam tries to find a cozy rug.
Tide pools laugh, making bubbles so sweet,
The beach balls bounce, oh what a treat!

Seashell selfies, everyone's in line,
With a wink and a wave, "This filter's divine!"
A frisbee flew, oh where did it land?
Caught up in laughter, as we run on sand.

With tales of the sea and whispers of breeze,
The giggles chase us with every tease.
So take off your shoes, let your worries drift,
In shadows and sun, all spirits uplift!

Lullabies of the Endless Blue

Lullabies sung by the waves at play,
A fishy choir leads the end of day.
Starfish think they're world-class stars,
In pajamas designed by "Tide and Bars."

The sunset dips, with a wink it goes,
While crabs on the shore wear sparkly clothes.
Anemones sway, dancing on their feet,
As sea turtles hum their favorite beat.

In the distance, a clam starts to snore,
As dolphins giggle, "Let's give them more!"
The sea whispers tales of dreams to unfold,
With giggles and chuckles, a wonder to hold.

So lean back and watch the moon's carefree flight,
While stars twinkle softly, oh what a sight.
The lullabies of now sway us to sleep,
In the arms of the ocean, secrets we keep.

The Rustle of Leaves

In the trees, a whisper plays,
Leaves giggle in the gentle sway,
Squirrels dance, a comic show,
Chasing tails as breezes blow.

A fruit drops, thuds on the ground,
A startled bird looks all around,
Nature's prankster, that ol' tree,
Hiding acorns for all to see.

Footsteps crunch on the forest floor,
A raccoon peeks from behind the door,
He snickers at the human plight,
While shadows play in fading light.

As night falls, the crickets sing,
To the tune of a leaf's soft fling,
Laughter mingles with the breeze,
Nature's quirks bring giggles with ease.

The Sigh of Seas

The waves tell jokes to the sandy shore,
A sea gull chuckles, then asks for more,
With every splash, a story's spun,
Mirthful tides beneath the sun.

Fish leap high, a graceful flip,
As if they've taken a comedy trip,
Crabs scuttle sideways, full of sass,
Strutting their stuff, they make quite the class.

A child waves at dolphins frolic,
While clowns in shells create a frolic,
The seaweed sways with an upbeat laugh,
Telling the tide to stay on the path.

When twilight comes, the colors blend,
The oceans giggle, they never end,
With every wave, another jest,
In the sea's embrace, all are blessed.

Verses at the Water's Edge

With sandy toes, the laughter flows,
A bucket spills, that's how it goes,
Seashells joke beneath our feet,
In rhythms light, they can't be beat.

A dog runs wild, a splashing scene,
Barking joyfully, oh so keen,
Chasing waves as they retreat,
Tripping over summer heat.

Picnics spread out, ants join the fun,
Stealing crumbs, they know they're on the run,
A seagull swoops, the sandwich flies,
While everyone shares surprised eyes.

As sun dips low, the day concludes,
The shoreline brims with carefree moods,
A once quiet edge now full of cheer,
Echoes of fun we hold most dear.

The Call of Lonely Coastlines

The cliffs stand tall with a wink of the sun,
Whispering secrets of adventures begun,
Seagulls gather, cackling free,
Plotting mischief by the sea.

Each wave that crashes tells a tall tale,
Of pirates lost and a ship's last sail,
The rocks chuckle at history's lore,
As crabs throw parties on the ocean floor.

Old driftwood lounges, in quiet repose,
With tales of travelers nobody knows,
A flip-flop's journey, a sock adrift,
Gifting laughter, a light-hearted gift.

The moonlight dances on watery lanes,
Chasing shadows, ignoring the pains,
A coastline sings with a cheeky glee,
Forever a stage, wild and free.

The Cadence of Breaking Surf

The surf rolls in with a comical sound,
Like giggles erupting all around,
Each crest a frothy, bubbly grin,
Inviting us all to dive right in.

Boys in shorts give a splashy cheer,
As girls with waves in their hair appear,
Bodies tumbling in a playful sea,
Nature's playground, it's pure esprit.

Sandcastles crumble, they wipe their brow,
"The tide's too strong," they take a bow,
But laughter echoes with the tide's resound,
For memories are the best gifts found.

When the sun sets low, the colors collide,
The surf lags slow with a humorous glide,
Each wave a whisper, soft and light,
In the salty air, all feels just right.

Echoes from the Forgotten Dock

A rusty old boat, creaking with glee,
Said, "Do you hear that? It's calling for me!"
The fish all around started cracking a smile,
And laughed at the boat, quite stuck in denial.

Seagulls squawked loudly, plotting their heist,
"Steal the captain's lunch, oh wouldn't that be nice?"
But the captain stood firm, holding on tight,
To his soggy old sandwich, a humorous sight!

Tangled seaweed danced, oh what a show,
While crabs on the shore argued, "Who's the star of the show?"
One dug in the sand, declared he'd be king,
But tripped on his claws, and fell with a fling.

At sunset they laughed, the sailors and fish,
"Who knew the dock could fulfill such a wish?"
As laughter bounced back from the water so deep,
The echoes of joy, they'd always keep.

Chants of the Tide-locked Spirits

Whispers of seafoam sang through the night,
Ghosts of the past caught in soft moonlight.
They giggled and twirled in the salty breeze,
Pretending to dance, like waves on the seas.

One spirit complained, "I lost my old hat!"
The others just laughed, "You look fine, how 'bout that?"
"But it had a great feather, tall and so proud!"
They all took a moment to laugh quite loud.

They reminisced tales of storms they survived,
Between bursts of laughter, together they thrived.
"I tripped on a whale, and fell with a splash!"
"Your socks, dear friend, did that really clash?"

As dawn broke, they faded with morning's soft rays,
Yet their laughter lingered to brighten our days.
So if you hear chuckles when the tides roll in,
Know it's those rascals, just up for a spin.

Footprints in the Forgotten Surf

Tiny feet on the sand, what a silly sight,
Running from waves, escaping the fright.
Little ones giggled, splashing with cheer,
While crabs danced around, with no hint of fear.

"Look, I left my mark!" one child exclaimed,
A crab gave a shrug, then scuttled, half-named.
"Your prints are quite cute, but check out these claws!"
The kids just roared with laughter and applause.

The tide rolled in fast, like a jokester's prank,
Washing away all that little feet spank.
"Hey! Come back!" they cried, as bubbles burst forth,
Even the ocean was chuckling, of course.

Yet footprints, like laughter, they always return,
With each playful wave, there's more fun to learn.
So dance on the shore, embrace every splash,
In the world of the surf, let your giggles clash!

Murmurs Beneath the Palms

Under palm fronds, where secrets conspire,
The whispers of coconuts stirred up the fire.
"Did you hear what she said?" the leaves foraged on,
"She swayed in the breeze till the sunshine was gone!"

A crab lounged nearby, with a grin oh-so-wide,
"All this chatter is fine, but come taste my tide!"
The shells shifted closer, intrigued by the song,
Together they giggled, all merry and strong.

The sun dipped low, and shadows grew tall,
While the beach threw a party, inviting them all.
A conch blew a horn, and the breeze joined in,
Creating a symphony, the night wore a grin.

The coconuts chuckled, sharing tales from afar,
Of party-hopping dolphins, who danced 'neath the stars.
With laughter like music, they spread with delight,
Murmurs beneath palms, keeping spirits bright.

The Ghosts of Nautical Footsteps

Ghosts waltz on the deck, so bold,
With boots made of seaweed, oh so old.
They slip and slide while doing a jig,
Their sails flapping like a large, weird pig.

The captain chuckles, a rum in hand,
As the crew tries to take a stand.
But every step leads to a splash,
A comical sight, a nautical clash.

The parrot laughs from its lofty perch,
Repeating jokes with a squawking lurch.
"Arrr, watch your step!" it cries with glee,
As the ghostly crew tumbles into the sea.

With echoes of laughter, the night wears thin,
These nautical ghosts have a wild spin.
They're the life of the party, it seems so true,
Even dead sailors know how to boo-hoo.

Echoing Whispers of Celestial Nights

Stars whisper secrets, but who can tell?
One says it's a joke, another, a spell.
They giggle and sparkle, a mischievous crew,
Plotting big capers with the moon in view.

The moon rolls its eyes, a celestial tease,
"Come dance with me, if you please!"
But the stars just twinkle, too fat to comply,
"Last time I danced, I fell from the sky!"

They plot to trick comets, a celestial race,
With whoopee cushions sent into space.
As meteors zoom with a whoosh and a blast,
Starry laughter echoes, a night unsurpassed.

Falling far too close, a comet says, "Oops!"
It spills all its stardust, creating some hoops.
In the laughter of night, they twinkle and flirt,
In the universe's joke, there's laughter and mirth.

Moonlight on Waters Uncharted

Moonlight dances like a quirky fish,
With dreams that twist into a strange dish.
Everyone watches with a wide-eyed stare,
As it juggles the waves without a care.

"Hey, what's this shimmer?" a sailor exclaims,
"Might be a concert of tricky sea games."
So they gather round, each one taking bets,
While the moon tries stand-up, a huge threat.

Crabs in tuxedos take front row seats,
With claps of their claws, they shuffle their feet.
The barnacles cheer with their hardened shells,
"Tell us another, we'll laugh 'til it swells!"

At dawn's approach, the humor runs dry,
As the fish dive deep, we bid them goodbye.
Yet the moon's jokes linger, splashed on the tide,
In the uncharted waters where funny most reside.

Flickers of Hope in the Surf

Waves crash with giggles, a tickle of foam,
Sending sandcastles back to their home.
Little crabs dart, playing hide and seek,
While the surf sings softly, distinct and cheeky.

A starfish grins with its five-pointed face,
"Watch me do flips, just give me some space!"
But it belly-flops wildly with each little wave,
Leaving the beach to cheer and misbehave.

Seagulls join in, cawing jokes from above,
"Who let the crab dance? It's just full of love!"
With each salty gust, the laughter grows loud,
As the surfers unite in a goofy crowd.

Yet hope's in the surf, in each playful crest,
With whispers of joy, it never can rest.
So dip your toes in, and come join the fun,
In the flickers of surf where laughter's begun.

Shadows of Forgotten Boats

A ship ran aground, oh what a sight,
The captain still swears he was not in fright.
His crew drank the rum, sang pirate songs,
While seagulls debated where each one belongs.

The sails turned to tents for mischief and play,
As crabby old crustaceans danced all day.
The hulls held secrets of fish gossip and jest,
While starfish pondered who looked the best.

The lighthouse blinked twice, inquiring with glee,
If boats could wear hats, what style might they see?
With flippers and fins, they'd strut on the beach,
While bored old barnacles gave lessons to teach.

So if you hear laughter near tangled old nets,
It's just boats being silly without any debts.
They weren't lost at sea, they just took a break,
To soak up the sun and a big piece of cake.

The Hidden Soundscape of Paradise

Listen closely, hear the coconuts chime,
As monkeys attempt to keep perfect time.
With whistles and clicks, crabs learn to boast,
While turtles partake in a conch shell toast.

The waves crash like jokes in a comedic play,
While parakeets squawk, just to brighten the day.
When coconut husks tumble with giggles galore,
It's a party where even the waves beg for more.

The islanders dance to a tropical beat,
And flip-flops are rhythmically tapping their feet.
As fish swish by with a flair of their tail,
They join in the fun, leaving bubbles to trail.

So if you find music when the sun's shining bright,
It's not just a dream, it's a tropical night.
With laughter and splashes, the echoes will stay,
In this hidden soundscape, we dance and play.

Resonance of the Coral Dreams

Beneath the waves where the sea fans grow,
Coral holds secrets that only fish know.
They whisper sweet tales in colors so bright,
As octopuses juggle late into the night.

With starry-eyed fishes, they gather and scheme,
To paint the sea floor in a colorful dream.
They caper and clown, a real underwater show,
While dolphins drift by, shouting, "Let's go!"

The anemones giggle and wave as they sway,
While sea cucumbers hide, "We can't join the play!"
But who needs a partner when bubbles abound,
And laughter erupts in the currents around?

So join in the dance, bring your fins and your flair,
In a symphony sung with salt in the air.
For every small creature, large dreams come alive,
In the resonance where all the fun thrives.

Memories within the Salt Air

Captured in laughter, the gulls swirl and glide,
While sunburned tourists take turns for the ride.
The beach ball bounced high, then bounced back real low,

A marvelous mess turning sand into show.

The surfcarpets rolled as surfers would cheer,
With tales of big waves that grew more unclear.
Each splash held a giggle, each dive was a blast,
As friends raced the tide, all too eager to last.

Shells piled like wishes, each one a delight,
As kids chased the crabs wearing hats in mid-flight.
With sunscreen applied like a coat of dear armor,
They'd wish for more days, oh, how they'd barter!

So treasure the moments, this salty affair,
Where memories linger, floating smooth in the air.
With giggles and sunshine, let joy be our guide,
As we dance with the breezes, side by side.

The Language of Shells and Stones

On the shore, shells gossip loud,
Each crack sharp, like laughter's crowd.
Stones chuckle, rolling with the tide,
Whispering secrets, they cannot hide.

A crab sidesteps, dancing all around,
With a top hat made of kelp he's found.
The starfish claps in a zen-like trance,
Inviting all to join the dance.

Seagulls squawk, the jesters of the air,
Dropping their snacks without a care.
Fish below, they just can't believe,
How talented the gulls can be!

So come, my friends, to this sandy place,
Join in the laughter, join the race.
In the language of shells, we laugh, we play,
Under the sun, we shout hooray!

Harmonies of the Distant Waters

The waves play music, a bubbly tune,
Like dolphins giggling beneath the moon.
Seashell trumpets sound a funny blast,
While fish dance like they had too much cast.

Mermaids sing, their voices a whirl,
Join in the fun, give a twirl!
A crab with a hat lifts up his claws,
Declaring himself king with such silly flaws.

The sand, oh the sand, a slippery floor,
Tripping all who come ashore.
With every splash, a chuckle erupts,
As seagulls dive with snack-filled cups.

So let the ocean's harmony play,
As laughter and joy fill the day.
The waters may call, but we must remain,
Dancing to music, we can't explain!

Fables Carried by the Ocean Wind

Whispers of tales ride gusty flares,
The wind tells jokes, no one really cares.
A wave rolls in, with a splash and a grin,
"Did you hear the one about the fish kin?"

Crabby sage sits atop a stone,
With his flaky skin, he's never alone.
His tales of woe are funny yet sad,
Of the one fish caught shivering in plaid.

Frisbees of seaweed are soaring high,
Flying past gulls, who huff with a sigh.
The sun beams down, a spotlight it seems,
On fish who dance in ridiculous dreams.

So let's gather 'round with laughter and cheer,
For the fables the wind carries are crystal clear.
Embrace the joy, and the tales shared anew,
In a world where humor is free for you!

Glimmers of Light on Still Waters

In still waters, the sun says hello,
Winking at frogs who put on a show.
A fish glides by, with a top hat so fine,
Quipping to lilies, "You're simply divine!"

Reflections twinkle like stars come alive,
As snails race by, trying hard to survive.
The reeds sway gently, in rhythm and rhyme,
"Catch me if you can!" is their playful chime.

Dragonflies hover, a circus in flight,
Trying to juggle, but they catch some fright.
A plop! A splash! And the laughter erupts,
As frogs applaud, while one of them jumps.

So let's all gather by these waters so bright,
Where glimmers of joy put our fears to flight.
With each ripple, let laughter expand,
In this playful paradise, hand in hand!

Notes from the Ocean's Embrace

A crab on the beach danced with glee,
His rhythm, like waves, was wild and free.
He tripped on a shell, let out a loud yelp,
Then scurried away, like it was just kelp.

Seagulls were laughing, swooping on down,
Stealing a sandwich from a frowning clown.
With mayo and mustard flying up high,
The seabreeze took off, and so did the rye!

The dolphin splashed water, much to our shock,
He wore a bright hat, tickling the block.
His joke about fish made everyone cheer,
But the octopus grumbled, "I can't drink beer!"

As sunset drew near, the whales told a joke,
About mermaids who danced and sometimes choke.
We laughed till we cried at the day's lovely chase,
In this comical sea, we all found our place.

Voices of the Shimmering Sands

In the sun, there danced a silly old crab,
Saying, "I'm king, can I sit in your gab?"
With a pinch and a smirk, he stole all the glory,
While the starfish just sighed, "Oh, tell me a story."

A turtle named Larry wore shades oh-so-fine,
He claimed he was cool, but we laughed at his line.
He waddled in style, but tripped on a stone,
And shouted, "Watch out! I'm still on my throne!"

The sandcastle teetered, a hurricane spun,
A kid with a bucket just laughed and had fun.
As the castle crumbled, a king made of sand,
Declared, "Let's rebuild! I've a shovel in hand!"

A seagull above squawked a tune with delight,
He carried a fish, oh what a great sight!
As we gathered around, took our turns to sing,
The comedy lingered, oh what joy it did bring!

Secrets in the Coral Quiet

Beneath the waves where the fish like to play,
A clownfish did joke in a most fishy way.
His friends rolled their eyes, but one gave a shout,
"Your puns are so bad, we're swimming right out!"

starfish and seaweed lured all in a dance,
They swayed with the currents, lost in a trance.
But there came a crab, scuttling in with a grin,
"Mind the bump, guys, it's a wild ocean spin!"

Anemones giggled, tickling schools that swam,
While a blowfish puffed up, "I'm the real jam!"
But as he got stuck, and couldn't deflate,
The fish gathered 'round, "Let's see how you're great!"

In the quiet of coral, where laughter was found,
Each creature had tales that echoed around.
These secrets of fun, in the depths they would bloom,
In the coral's embrace, we forget all our gloom!

Serenade of the Ebbing Tide

With the tide rolling back, we heard a loud cheer,
A jellyfish jiggled, said, "Look, I'm quite near!"
He bounced to the rhythm of waves and the breeze,
While we doubled over, gasping at ease.

A fish in a tutu swam past with a flair,
While dolphins played chess, tossing fish in the air.
"Checkmate!" one shouted, with a flip and a twist,
The laughter erupted; there was much to be missed!

Sand dollars whispered their secrets out loud,
As crabs on the shore formed a comical crowd.
"Oh please, do tell us, what's your grand skill?"
They said, "We just scuttle, but it gives us a thrill!"

As the sun kissed the sea and night claimed its throne,
We sang to the stars, with voices our own.
In the serenade sweet that the ocean had spun,
We found all our laughter—the night had begun!

Heartbeats of a Hidden Paradise

In the shade of a coconut tree,
A crab danced with utmost glee.
It waved its tiny claw with pride,
As tourists watched, laughter amplified.

The parrot squawked a cheeky jest,
While sunbathers took a nap and rest.
A flip-flop flew, a sight so clear,
Chased by a dog, full of cheer.

Shells whispered secrets to the shore,
While a starfish played a game of war.
The tide rolled in with a giggle and tease,
As flip-flops floated like leaves in a breeze.

Bikini woes and ice cream spills,
Brought extra laughter, courtesy of thrills.
In this paradise, quirky and bright,
Every heartbeat felt just right!

Cascades of Time on Driftwood

Driftwood logs told tales of yore,
While seagulls squabbled, swooping for more.
A raccoon in shades, looking quite cool,
Auditions for 'Starfish' at the beach school.

Sandcastles rose like towers of might,
Only to fall in the next sunset light.
Kids in despair, but oh what a blast,
They built them again, learning fast.

A pelican dived with a belly flop,
Making the sunbathers laugh till they stop.
Buckets and spades, a joyous parade,
Every minute here, a memory made.

Time cascaded like waterfalls near,
With jests echoing, loud and clear.
In driftwood's embrace, laughter ran free,
In this whimsical patch of the sea.

The Sound of Waves Embracing Solitude

Waves whispered secrets to lonely sands,
While a hermit crab plotted, making plans.
It wore a tiny shell with flair,
Strutting as if it had no care.

The clams all giggled beneath their rock,
As a seagull laughed and took stock.
Meanwhile, a flip-flop floated away,
Claiming independence on that day.

A lone coconut rolled up and down,
Catching sunbathers, creating a frown.
But a dolphin could not resist the tease,
Flipping and flopping with effortless ease.

Solitude sang a funny little tune,
As fish danced beneath the watchful moon.
The waves kept chortling, a merry salute,
As life played on, with whimsical pursuit.

Serenade of the Moonlit Lagoon

The lagoon shimmered like a stage,
Where frogs croaked tales of a different age.
A firefly twinkled, trying to impress,
While a misfit crab danced in a dress.

Moonlight's gaze caught fish so sly,
Who swam in loops, oh so spry.
A turtle giggled, lost in the show,
As laughter echoed, filling the flow.

A boat drifted by, with snacks to share,
But seagulls swooped in with gusto and flair.
They snatched the nachos, much to dismay,
As the crew burst into laughter, ready to play.

Nestled beneath stars, the night grew bold,
With every chuckle, a tale to unfold.
In this lagoon, where quirks intertwine,
The serenade lingers, timeless and fine.

The Voyage of Lost Whispers

A boat made of jelly and dreams,
Sailed by the fish, or so it seems.
With giggles that dance on the waves,
We search for the treasure, mischief braves.

Crabs in tuxedos, a waltz on the shore,
While seagulls critique our song's encore.
We laugh as the tide takes our snacks away,
Oh, the price we pay for a sunlit day!

A parrot's squawk is our captain's clue,
Spinning tall tales while sipping on dew.
A map drawn in ketchup reveals the way,
To find the lost whispers and win the day!

As night falls, we tell tales of the brave,
Of mermaids who dance in the ocean's wave.
The laughter that echoes is never to fade,
As we drift off to sleep in our jelly parade.

Breeze-Kissed Memories of the Past

Whispers of laughter ride on the breeze,
Old beach towels dancing with such carefree ease.
We chase after ghosts in flip-flop attire,
While cantaloupe crabs try to steal our fire.

Forgotten sun hats sit on the sand,
Hiding secret wishes made by the hand.
Sandcastles topple with playful might,
When gulls swoop down for a midnight bite.

Seashells gossip about who's misconstrued,
Dramas unfold in the crabby old brood.
Like beach ball shenanigans lost in a dive,
We dance with the memories, feeling alive!

The sun paints a picture at the close of day,
While the tide drags away all worries and fray.
With giggles and breezes, we bask in the past,
In a world where the fun is meant to last.

Treasures Buried Under the Stars

At midnight, we dig for treasures untold,
With chocolate gold coins, our fortunes unfold.
The stars twinkle secrets, a riddle divine,
That leads us to laughter, our shared straight line.

Flipping beach mats to cover our finds,
Giggling at shadows, we tease silly minds.
With maps drawn in jelly and pens made of sand,
We unearth the smiles that were perfectly planned.

A dragonfly digs with a wink of its eye,
While we ponder if donuts can really fly high.
With every soft chuckle, the moon shares a grin,
As we dance on the sands, letting fun now begin.

In a patch of bright starlight, we discover our fate,
A chest full of giggles, but we'll never be late.
To claim treasures buried, with friends at our side,
In this whimsical night, we laugh, we abide.

Currents of Forgotten Tales

A wave crashes softly, a giggle afloat,
Where tales of the sea ride a whimsical boat.
Octopus scribbles with ink made of foam,
As we wander in circles, far away from home.

Seashells spin yarns of the fish they once met,
Like Ivan the Incredible, who never forgets.
When mermaids wear socks to hide shiny tails,
And dolphins recite their patty-cake tales.

We sway with the stories, like kites in the air,
While waves tickle toes with smooth, salty flair.
The sand tickles our thoughts with each playful mound,
As legends of laughter echo all around.

So let's pool our echoes, our tales and our fun,
Under the moon, as the bright day is done.
With currents that whisper of giggles we tell,
We sail on through laughter, where all is quite well!

Traces of Elysian Winds

There once was a breeze with a laugh,
It tickled the trees, oh what a gaffe.
It blew off my hat,
And flung it to Pat,
Who thought it was lunch, what a chaff!

The clouds rolled in, played a prank,
Dancing around like a mischievous prank.
They rained down confetti,
And the gulls got all sweaty,
Screaming, 'What's this? It's no plank!'

The sun peeked out with a grin,
Said, 'Let the fun games begin.'
It warmed up the sea,
Made jellyfish flee,
While mermaids played cards, oh the din!

We laughed with the waves in a whirl,
As they tumbled and danced with a twirl.
That salty spray dare,
Got caught in my hair,
Now I'm the head of a seaweed girl!

Motions of the Undulating Sea

The sea danced around with delight,
Making waves that splashed left and right.
A fish in a tux,
With bubbles and flux,
Thought he'd join in for a night.

Crabs took a break from their sand,
Waltzing and clapping their claws on the strand.
They threw a small bash,
Complete with a splash,
While snails tried to lead—oh, how they planned!

With seaweed as garland and crown,
The surf grinned like it wore a brown gown.
A turtle rolled through,
With jokes tried and true,
Spinning tales that brought giggles abound.

We gathered at dusk for a laugh,
As dolphins put on a grand staff.
They leaped and they spun,
In mischief and fun,
Oh, the motions were quite the gaff!

Spheres of Stillness Beneath the Foam

Beneath the surface, things poked fun,
An octopus juggling just one.
With arms in a twist,
He waved with a fist,
Each ball said, 'Who's our number one?'

The starfish played cards with a crab,
But lost to a clambake celebrity fab.
They gambled with shells,
And told silly tells,
While seahorses laughed at the blab.

Anemones swayed with a flair,
Telling secrets that curled in the air.
They whispered to fish,
"Wouldn't it be swish,
If we all wore hats made of hair?"

So all of the sea creatures guffawed,
At the silly things nature had rawed.
For beneath the deep blue,
With giggles in view,
The ocean felt like a grand façade!

Wind Homilies Under Hidden Skies

The wind told a tale of surprise,
As it swooped in with mischievous eyes.
It tickled a tree,
And sent a kite free,
While whispers echoed soft 'neath the skies.

A flock of birds joined in the jest,
With feathers and flaps, they felt blessed.
They chirped loud and clear,
In rhythms sincere,
And made the shy clouds feel impressed.

The gusts stirred up laughter and cheer,
As they swirled 'round with nothing to fear.
They blew hats off folks,
And shared silly jokes,
While everyone danced with good beer!

So here's to the wind's playful art,
Creating a world full of heart.
Underneath its embrace,
We find joyful space,
Where wind-whispers dance—a fine part!

www.ingramcontent.com/pod-product-compliance
Lightning Source LLC
Chambersburg PA
CBHW072222070526
44585CB00015B/1454